One of the most important people in Jami's life was her grandfather, Poppy. Jami really looked up to Poppy and always listened to what he had to say. He had much wisdom about life and about growing up. And whenever Jami had a problem, Poppy always had the answer.

Jami enjoyed spending time with her grandfather, Poppy.

The Blizzard

In December of 1987, Jami went snow skiing with her friend Lisa Barzano. They skied in the mountains of Colorado. On the way home, they were caught in the middle of a terrible **blizzard**.

The blinding snow was falling so thickly that Jami couldn't see. Jami took a wrong turn, and the car became stuck in the snow. Within a few hours, the two girls were **stranded**.

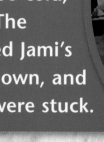

If a car gets too cold, it won't run. The blizzard caused Jami's car to break down, and she and Lisa were stuck.

Jami and Lisa were trapped in the car for 11 days. No one knew what had happened to them. The snow was too high for them to walk in, so they could not go looking for help.

A cinnamon bun and a bag of peanuts were all they had to eat. The only thing they had to drink was melted snow.

Blizzards can be dangerous if you aren't protected from the cold. The winds howl, and the temperature can fall below 0° Fahrenheit.

The girls also didn't have any blankets to keep them warm. They had to put on all the clothes they had with them. Their shoes were wet and cold, so ski boots were the only things they had to cover their feet. Their toes and legs began to get **hypothermia**.

But no matter what, they never lost hope.

Search teams use dogs, helicopters, and snowmobiles to find people lost in the snow.

Rescued!

Finally, on January 2, 1988, Jami and Lisa were rescued. Two men were out riding their snowmobiles, and they saw the car buried in the snow. They called the search teams for help. Soon, the girls were rushed to the hospital.

That was not the end of their troubles, however. Jami's feet and legs were badly injured from the cold. Lisa also spent several weeks in the hospital. There were still some hard times ahead for the both of them.

Healing Time

Jami spent the next several weeks in the hospital. The doctors were worried because her feet had very bad **frostbite**. The frostbite caused a very bad **infection** in her feet.

As time went on, Jami's feet and legs were not getting better. She had many

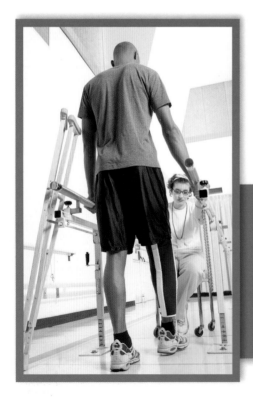

operations. The doctors worked hard to fight the infection in her feet, but nothing helped.

Many people who have had a very bad injury to their arms or legs need physical therapy to help them move well again.

The doctors decided that Jami would have to have both of her legs **amputated**. This is an operation in which the doctors remove the part of the body that is sick and cannot get better.

On January 24, 1988, Jami's legs were amputated six inches below each knee. Even though she lost a large part of her legs, this operation saved Jami's life. Without it, the frostbite infection would have spread to other parts of her body.

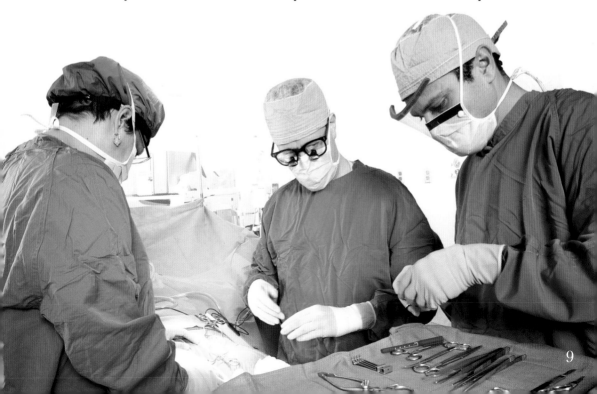

Jami felt very scared after the operation. Would she ever be able to ski, or wear shoes, or dance again?

Poppy visited her often. He reminded her that her family loved her. He also said, "You still have your life. You need to make the best of it."

Jami had never really exercised much before. She didn't really like to. But Poppy told her that she would have to exercise if her body was going to get healthy and strong once again.

People with prosthetic arms and legs can still run and play sports.

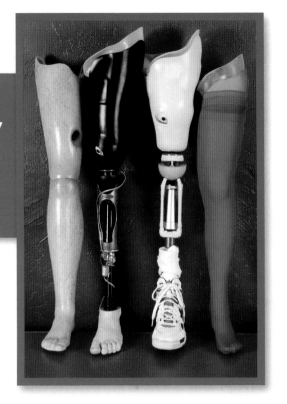

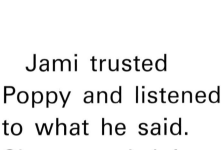
Prosthetic legs are made in many different shapes and sizes for all kinds of people.

Jami trusted Poppy and listened to what he said. She started doing the physical therapy exercises the doctors gave her to do. She also got **prosthetic** legs, which are metal and plastic legs that would help her to walk. On February 19, 1988, Jami walked out of the hospital on her new legs.

The years passed, and Jami finished college and got a job. Life seemed to return to normal.

Running with Cheetah Legs

In November of 1996, Poppy died. Jami missed her grandfather very much. That same year Jami began watching the Paralympics on TV. The Paralympics are sports games for people with **physical disabilities**.

Poppy had always told Jami to never give up. To honor his memory, Jami decided that she would start running.

Hockey is one of the many games played in the Paralympics.

Getting Started

Jami wanted something that would help her run really fast. Her doctor suggested a new type of prosthetic legs called "cheetah legs." These were special legs made just for running. Jami decided to give them a try.

The cheetah legs didn't look like other prosthetic legs. They looked more like metal hooks. And they were very bouncy.

Jami noticed a big difference between running in these cheetah legs and running in her prosthetic legs.

Cheetahs are the fastest land animals on Earth. They can run up to 70 miles per hour. Jami couldn't run quite that fast, but the cheetah legs helped her run faster than she ever had before.

Jami worked out with her new legs every day. Soon, she was ready for her first race.

Cheetah legs don't look like other prosthetic legs, but they help people run like star athletes.

In April of 1997, Jami ran her first 100 meter race. The cheetah legs worked great! She ran much faster than she thought she could, and she came in fourth place.

Jami really enjoyed running. She exercised more and more. And while she trained, she often thought of Poppy and the words of encouragement he'd given her.

The Winning Edge

Jami began racing with the cheetah legs in the spring of 1997. She ran against other **double amputees** from all over the world. She ran races in the United States, Germany, England, and Australia.

Jami's Races Around the World

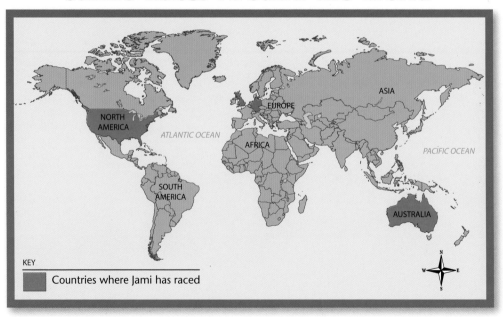

KEY

■ Countries where Jami has raced

16

Over time, Jami got faster and faster. She won many gold medals. She loved racing so much, she decided to become a professional runner.

Jami became the world's fastest female double amputee in sprint races. These sprint races are very short. In 1999, she set the world record for the 100 meter and 400 meter races.

Today, Jami is a role model to many people. In 1999, Jami was named the U.S. Disabled Woman of the Year. And in 2003, she received an honor from the America's Athletes with Disabilities Association.

Jami tells her story to large crowds all over the country. She tells them about the 11 days she spent trapped in the snow. She also tells them how she stayed positive and worked hard to reach her goals.

Jami has received many awards in her lifetime.

Finishing First

As a runner and a speaker, Jami wants people to know that no matter how difficult life becomes, you must never give up.

Her grandfather Poppy was the first one to teach her this. He'd said, "You still have your life. You need to make the best of it."

And that's just what Jami did.

Jami listened to her grandfather's wise words, and she became very successful because of it.

Important Events in Jami's Life

December 23, 1987
Jami and Lisa get
stuck in a blizzard.

January 2, 1988
The girls are rescued.

1985   ○   ○   **1990**   **1995**

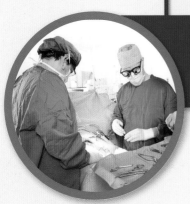

January 24, 1988
Jami has surgery to
remove her legs.

February 19, 1988
Jami walks out of the
hospital on prosthetic legs.

November, 1996
Grandfather Poppy dies.

April, 1997
Jami runs in her first 100 meter race and comes in fourth.

2003
Jami receives an honor from the America's Athletes with Disabilities Association.

O   O   ⅲⅲⅲ   O   **2000**   ⅲⅲⅲⅲⅲⅲ   O   ⅲⅲⅲ   **2005**

1999
Jami sets the world records in the 100 meter and 400 meter races.

1999
Jami is named U.S. Disabled Woman of the Year.

Glossary

amputate to remove a part of the body, such as an arm or leg

blizzard a very bad snowstorm with strong winds and thick snow

double amputee a person who has had either both arms or both legs removed

frostbite an injury to a part of the body caused by the cold

hypothermia when the body's temperature falls dangerously low

infection a sickness that spreads through part or all of the body

physical disability a problem with the body that keeps a person from doing everyday things

prosthetic something used to replace a missing body part

stranded to be left somewhere with no way to leave

Index

Running Free
The Jami Goldman Story

Claire Daniel

Contents

Rigby®
A Harcourt Achieve Imprint

www.Rigby.com
1-800-531-5015

Young Jami

Jami Goldman was born on November 21, 1968. She was like many other kids growing up. She loved reading, playing with her brother, and playing dodgeball. When Jami wasn't in school, she enjoyed playing at home. When her friends went out to the movies or to the mall, Jami often stayed behind. She liked it better when her friends came over to her house to play.

Jami enjoyed playing with her brother when she was young.